Diamond Sky

Diamond Sky

Jampa Thaye

Foreword
Karma Thinley Rinpoche

Ganesha Press
Bristol
1989

Ganesha Press Ltd.
27 Lilymead Ave
Knowle, Bristol
BS4 2BY

British Library Cataloguing in Publication Data
Thaye, Jampa, *1952* —
1. Buddhist life. Meditation
I. Title
294.3 '443

ISBN 0 9509119 1 7

Typeset and printed by Manchester Free Press

Revealing the body of Vajradhara,
Uttering the speech of **sūtra** *and* **mantra**
Perfectly encompassing with the mind of **mahāmudrā**
To Karma Thinleypa I bow down.

Karma Thinley Rinpoche, master of the Sakya and Kagyu traditions of Buddhism and founder of numerous *dharma*-centres in the United Kingdom and Canada.

Diamond Sky

CONTENTS

Illustrations

Padmakara / 30

*Padmakara, shown here in the form of Guru Lotus Blazing Light, is the great **Vajrayāna** master who established Buddhism in Tibet in the eighth century. Known as the 'Second Buddha of Oḍḍiyana', he is simultaneously the manifestation of the blessings of all Buddhas and the emanation of Buddha Amitābha. In this age of great defilements, he represents the unfailing refuge of the deathless buddha-nature.*

Milarepa / 42

*Milarepa was the second of the three founding patriarchs of the Kagyu tradition in Tibet. As a disciple of Marpa Lotsā-va, he inherited the full range of teachings transmitted by the Buddhist **tantric** masters of India. His life, as a cotton-clad yogin and hermit in the mountain fastnesses of Tibet and Nepal, has provided an unparalleled example of devotion and asceticism. His teachings, in the form of songs and poetry, remain as an unceasing inspiration to all generations of meditators.*

Sonam Tsemo / 52

*Sonam Tsemo was the second of the five founding lamas of the Sakya tradition. Revered as an incarnation of the **bodhisattva** Mañjuśrī, his scholarly achievements and* *meditational attainments helped to endow the developing Sakya school with an immense vigour and creativity.*

Vajrayoginī / 72

Vajrayoginī, shown here in the form of Nāro Ḍākinī, is one of the principal deities of **Vajrayāna** *Buddhism. In particular, her meditational cycle belongs to the mother* **tantra** *class of* **anuttara tantra.** *As the embodiment of the luminous and empty nature of mind she liberates all conceptual activity in the space of enlightened energy.*

Mahākāla / 89

Shown here in the form of Gonpo Gur as propitiated in the Sakya tradition, **Mahākāla** *is the chief protector of the* **dharma.** *As the embodiment of the activity of all the Buddhas, he guards the energy of the* **dharma** *from perversion and assists tantric yogins in their accomplishment of spiritual power.*

Illustrated by Rana Lister and Paul Salmon.

༄༈། འཛམ་བུ་གླིང་ལ་ཏོག་ལྷར་ལེགས་ཚོགས་དུ་མས་མངོ་བའི་ཕྲེན།

ཡུལ་རྒྱལ་ཁམས་ཉེན་པོ་ནས། དང་བཙོ་ཉེས་རབ་ཀྱི་སྒོས་དཔལ་མཐའ་ག། རང་སྟོན་

ཐུགས་ར་རྒྱམས་པ་མཐུན་ཡམ་ཀྱིས་བརྟམས་མཛད་པའི་ཉ་རས་པའི་ཚེས་ལ་འཇུག་

པའི་རྩལ་འདིས། ྃ་སྟོན་པ་བྲུབ་པའི་དངར་པོའི་རེ་ལྔགས་ལ་མ་བཟང་པོ་ལ་སྟོན་

གནེར་ུ་རྒྱིའི་བསྐལ་པ་བཟང་པོ་ཅན་ལ་ངོ་མ་ནོར་པའི་མིག་ སྙེ་བའི་ཡིད་ ཉེས་ཡོན་

པར་འུན་ཀྱིས་ཚོས་བརྩི་ལྒྱུ་བ་གལ་ཆེ་ཁ། ཉེས་པཝང་འདི་ལྱར་དགོས་ཉེས་སྒྲུ་

ཚ་ཐྱམས་པ་གང་ནས་གཟུང་འསྒྲུལ་ཐོ། མདོ་ཁམས་ཚོས་ཀྱིཞིང་སར་སྒྲེན་

པའི་བསྐལ་པ་དགེ་བ་ཅན། སྟོན་དང་བསྟན་པ་ལ་མི་ཕྱེད་པའི་དད་གུས་ར་ལྷུན་པ།

ྃ་མཛོན་ཁ་རྟོད་པར་འཆར་བའི་ལུང་གིས་ཀརྒྱ་ཕྱིན་ལས་བནི་མེར་པས། རབ་ཕྱུར་

བརྩུ་བཤུན་པའི་ྃ་ཚེས་དགེ་བར་ཕྲེབ

Foreword

This method of entering the holy *dharma* has been composed by my student Ngakpa Jampa Thaye, who is endowed with the glorious power of faith, energy and wisdom and comes from the kingdom of Great Britain, a country elevated through its many excellent qualities to resemble the peak of the world. Since those who have the good fortune of training in the excellent path of the tradition of Buddha Śākyamuni presented here will come to possess the eye of conviction which discriminates the unmistaken meaning, it is important that everyone should endeavour to study this teaching. Thus I request.

At the urging of my *dharma*-regent Jampa, I who have the virtuous good fortune of being born in the *dharma* country of Kham and possess undivided faith and devotion towards Lord Buddha and His doctrine, named the Fourth Karma Thinley by the authority of the one who holds the black crown, have written this at an auspicious date in the seventeenth cycle.

Introduction

AS A RESULT of numerous requests, I have composed this brief introduction to the practice of the three vehicles of Buddha: *hīnayāna, mahāyāna* and *vajrayāna.* Since it is based on the precepts of the great *dharma*-masters of India and Tibet transmitted to me by my gurus, I hope that it will inspire confidence, devotion and practice.

Nowadays, a growing number of people in the West are becoming interested in Buddha's teachings but success in accomplishing them depends upon a clear unmistaken knowledge of the essential points of practice. As Gyalsay Thogme says:

> 'Perfect Buddhas — source of all benefit and bliss
> Arise through cultivating the holy *dharma*
> And since this depends upon understanding its practices
> I shall explain those of a Conqueror's Child!'

Therefore I have tried to set forth in a simple, yet comprehensive, manner the objects and order of spiritual practice that lead one to the achievement of complete Buddhahood.

It is the meeting with a Buddhist guru who himself

represents a genuine lineage of spiritual transmission which first reveals to us the possibility of travelling the path. Thus, since confidence in the various lineages of transmission is of such key importance for the practitioner I have presented in Chapter I 'Discovering the Things that Remain', a brief account of the unfolding of *dharma* in India and Tibet, whence it is now spreading to the West.

In Chapter II, 'Solid Rock', I have outlined the significance of taking refuge, the fundamental commitment to the Buddhist spiritual path. In this commitment one recognises the guru and the three jewels of Buddha, *dharma* and *sangha* as the sustaining foundation of one's practice. However, although one has committed oneself to the spiritual life, the seductions and fears of the ephemeral yet potent play of worldly experiences can still entrap one. The antidote to such imprisonment is cultivation of authentic renunciation which dissolves the prison walls of our neuroses. In Chapter III, 'Tasting Birth and Death', the ever fresh teachings known as the 'four contemplations that turn the mind' are presented as the basis of such renunciation and thus as the quintessential teachings of the *hīnayāna*.

Chapters IV, 'Open Heart' and V 'The Crystal Key', focus on *bodhicitta* ('the thought of enlightenment'), the alchemical agent of spiritual transformation and essence of the *mahāyāna*. In 'Open Heart', I introduce the meditation precepts through which one can generate the unbounded compassion of *bodhicitta* that impels one to dedicate oneself to achieve Buddhahood in order to bring about the welfare and ultimate liberation of all suffering beings. Yet such compassion is incomplete without the wisdom aspect of *bodhicitta*. Hence, in the subsequent chapter 'The Crystal Key', I have presented calm-abiding and insight meditation out of which the recognition of the true nature of phenomena is born.

Finally, in Chapter VI, 'The Path of the Emperor', I have outlined the fundamental meaning and purpose of the teachings of the supreme vehicle, the *vajrayāna*. Since practice of this vehicle is so crucial, I have tried to show how one must cultivate the pure vision of the profound view, receive empowerment, maintain *samaya* and accomplish the various facets of the esoteric path. In this way, one is enthroned as Buddha Vajradhara, liberator of the entire ocean of sentient beings.

I cannot repay the peerless kindness of my Vajradhara guru, Karma Thinley Rinpoche, nor that of my other gurus such as H.H. Sakya Trizin and Phende Rinpoche, but this book is offered to them in devotion. Thanks also to the poetic lineage of Kerouac, Ginsberg and Dylan who, so many years ago, sparked it all off for me, and finally to my wife Ngawang Dolma for her unending support in this work, as in all others.

Ngakpa Jampa Thaye
3rd January, 1989

One

Discovering the things that remain

Through the greatest compassion
He knows the world.
Having seen all worlds,
Whilst never departing from the *Dharmakaya*,
Through various forms, apparitional by nature,
The One excellently born into the highest birth
Descends from Tusita
Enters the womb and is nobly born.
Perfectly skilled in all art and craft,
Taking delight in the company of his consorts,
He renounces the world and practises austerities.
Going to the 'Heart of Enlightenment',
He vanquishes the hosts of Mara —
Then — Perfect Enlightenment,
He turns the Wheel of *Dharma* and passes away
into *Nirvana*.[1]

THE HISTORY OF Buddhism begins with our matchless teacher Śākyamuni Buddha who was born some two thousand five hundred years ago in Lumbini, a place situated just inside the present day borders of Nepal. At the age of thirty-five, He attained enlightenment at Bodhgaya in India and then turned the wheel of *dharma* (the teachings) at Varanasi and various other locations. Finally, at the age of eighty, having spent His life teaching, He passed away at Kuṣinagara. In this way the door of liberation was opened.

Following Lord Buddha's passing, His teaching was

preserved in diverse lines of transmission, the first of which to flourish openly were those espousing the *hīnayāna* ('lesser vehicle') teachings. Although a total of eighteen *hīnayāna* sects are said to have existed in this early period, the most important were the *Sarvastivāda* and *Sthaviravāda*. The former sect is now extinct but the latter, known nowadays by its Pali name of *Theravāda*, still survives and is, in fact, the dominant form of Buddhism in south-east Asia.

The *mahāyāna* ('great vehicle') teachings, originally delivered by Lord Buddha to His *bodhisattva* disciples, both human and divine, began to spread widely from about the first century C.E. onwards. This occurred through the public dissemination of such *sūtras* ('discourses') as the Perfection of Wisdom. The two pre-eminent figures in the popularisation of the *mahāyāna* in India were the great philosophers Nāgārjuna and Asanga. Nāgārjuna was the originator of the *Mādhyamika* ('Middle Way') philosophical school which arose out of his teaching on emptiness, the profound meaning of the Perfection of Wisdom. Nāgārjuna's lineage was continued by his spiritual son Āryadeva. Two principal branches of the *Mādhyamika* subsequently developed in India: the *Svatantrika* represented by such masters as Bhavaviveka and Jñānagarbha, and the *Prasaṅgika* represented by Buddhapalita, Candrakīrti and Śāntideva.

Asanga, together with his brother Vasubandhu, established a second major *mahāyāna* philosophical school, that of the *Cittamatra* ('Mind-Only') or *Yogācāra*. This school focussed particularly on such *sūtras* as the Laṅkāvatāra and Sandhinirmocana, which explicated the function of mind as the basis for the appearance of the phenomenal world. In addition, Asanga himself received a series of five works through the visionary inspiration of the *bodhisattva* Maitreya. These five works, the

Abhisamayālaṃkāra, Mahāyānasūtra-laṃkāra, Dharma-dharmatā Vibhaṇga, Madhyānta Vibhāga and the *Uttaratantraśāstra* were known collectively as *'The Five Teachings of Maitreya'* and have been of great importance for all followers of the *mahāyāna*. Many later scholars hold these works to be *Cittamatra* in intent, but others such as the *gzhan-stong-pas* [2] have seen these as representing the view of the so-called 'Great *Madhyamaka*'.

Following the open manifestations of the *hīnayāna* and *mahāyāna*, a third major wave occurred between the fifth and tenth centuries C.E. with the spread of the *vajrayāna* or 'secret mantra' teachings. The *vajrayāna* originated in the esoteric teachings of Lord Buddha known as the *tantras*, which He had communicated to His most advanced disciples. These supremely precious teachings had then been preserved in great secrecy until the fifth century, from which time onwards they had begun to be revealed somewhat more openly. However, great caution and strictness were still exercised as to the suitability of the recipient. In the mediaeval period the most famous practitioners of the *vajrayāna* were the eighty-four *siddhas*, which group included such masters of *mahāmudrā* [3] as Virupā, Nāropā and Saraha.

The major movement of *dharma* to Tibet from India took place in two phases known as the periods of the 'early' and 'later' diffusions during which time the full range of *hīnayāna, mahāyāna* and *vajrayāna* teachings were transmitted to the Tibetans. The early diffusion commenced during the reign of King Srongtsen Gampo (Srong-btsan sGam-po) (d. 649 C.E.) and came to a climax in the reign of his descendant Trisrong Detsun (Khri Srong IDe brTsan (756-797)). At that time, Padmakara, the 'Precious Guru' from Oḍḍiyana, embodiment of the Buddhas of past, present and future, together with the Indian philosopher Śāntirakṣita, upholder of the unified Yogācāra Madhyamaka view, established the first Tibetan *dharma*-centre at Samye, south-west of Lhasa, and initiated the study and practice of the *sūtras* and *tantras.*

Furthermore, Padmakara, having transmitted the teaching of the *mahā, anu* and *ati*-yogas to his twenty-five foremost disciples such as Yeshe Tsogyal (Ye-shes mTsho-rgyal) concealed a vast number of esoteric instructions in cypher manuscript form in various places throughout Tibet. These have been discovered at the predicted times through the centuries by blessed emanations of himself known as 'treasure finders' (gter-ston).

From the activities of Padmakara and other great masters such as Vimalamitra and Vairocana, arose the first of the four major schools of Buddhism in Tibet: The Nying-ma ('Ancient') tradition. The principal teaching of this tradition is *ati* (rdzogs-chen)[4] the pinnacle of the nine-vehicle meditational system. Amongst the innumerable accomplished Nyingma teachers who have appeared in Tibetan history, perhaps the greatest was Longchen Rab-jam (kLong-chen Rab-'byams (1308-1363), whose numerous works contain the most complete and profound presentation of *ati.*

The 'later diffusion' of *dharma* in the tenth and eleventh centuries followed a period of confusion in Tibetan Buddhism due largely to the effect of the anti-Buddhist policies of the apostate king Langdarma (gLang Dar-ma) in the ninth century. This second diffusion coincided with, and was to some extent a product of, a series of new translations of *tantras* from India initiated by such scholars as Rinchen Zangpo (Rin-chen bZang-po) (958-1055) and Marpa Lotsava (Mar-pa Lotsā-va (1012-1096)). During this period, in addition to a number of lesser sects such as Chod-yul (gCod-yul) and Shangpa (Shangs-pa), three especially prominent schools, all following the new *tantras*, came into being: the Kadam (bKa'-gdams), the Kagyu (bKa'-brgyud) and the Sakya (Sa-skya).

The first of these, the Kadam school, traces its origins to the work of Atīśa (979-1054), who spent the last thirteen years of his life in Tibet. It was Atīśa's chief disciple Dromton ('brom-ston (1000-1064) who actually founded the sect and its first monastery at Radeng (Rwa-sgrengs). Subsequently the Kadampa teachings spread through central and western Tibet. The tradition possessed three lineages of transmission: 'treatise' (gzhung) consisting of six *mahāyāna* texts such as Śāntideva's *'Entering the Bodhisattva Conduct'*; 'oral instructions' (gdams-ngag) consisting of the mind-training (blo-sbyong) meditation-cycle, and 'pith-instructions' (man-ngag) comprising *tantric* teachings such as the famous *'Four Deities of the Kadam'*, Śākyamuni, Avalokiteśvara, Green Tāra and Acala.

The Kadam alone, of the major new *tantric* schools, has not survived as an independent sect although its teachings have been absorbed into the other traditions of Tibetan Buddhism. In the fourteenth and fifteenth centuries Mañjuśrī Tsong Khapa (gTsong Kha-pa 1357-1419) established the Gelug (dGe-lugs) or Gandenpa (dGa'-ldan-pa) sect which, in certain respects, might be called 'the new Kadam'. Thanks to Tsong Khapa and other brilliant scholars such as Gyaltsab (rGyal-tshab 1364-1432) and Khedrup-je (mKhas-grub rJe (1385-1483), the Gelugpa tradition has been particularly renowned not only for its emphasis on monastic discipline but also for its specialisation in logic. In addition, from 1649 until modern times, the Gelugpa enjoyed political power in Tibet through the office of the successive incarnations of the Dalai Lama, hierarch of the monastery of Drepung, ('bras-spungs), emanation of Avalokiteśvara and King of Tibet.

The second of the major new *tantric* schools

established in Tibet in the eleventh century was the
Kagyu tradition of Marpa Lotsa. Marpa received, from his
Indian gurus Nāropā and Maitrīpā, *mahāmudrā* and the
'six doctrines'[5] which subsequently became the most
famous Kagyupa teachings. Marpa's principal disciple was
the yogin and poet Milarepa (Mi-la ras-pa 1040-1123) who
in turn transmitted the lineage to the Kadampa monk
Gampopa (sGam-po-pa 1079-1153). It was Gampopa, also
known as Dakpo Lhaje (Dwags-po Lha-rje), who by blen-
ding together the *mahāmudrā* teaching of Milarepa and
the *sūtra* teachings of the Kadampa into one stream, endowed the Kagyu tradition both with its characteristic
doctrinal and institutional forms and its proper name
'Dakpo Kagyu' (Dwags-po bKa'-brgyud).

Following Gampopa the tradition, transmitted
through his four principal disciples, split into four major
branches, the Phakmo Dru (Phag-mo Gru), the Tshal
(Tshal) of Lama Zhang (Zhang), the Baram ('ba'-ram) of
Baram Dorje Wangchuk ('ba'-ram rDo-rje dBang-phyug),
and the Karma of Karma-pa Dusum Khyenpa (Dus-gsum
mKhyen-pa). The first of these, issuing from the great
meditator Phakmo Dru Dorje Gyaltsen (Phag-mo Gru rDo-
rje rGyal-mtshan (1110-1170) engendered in its turn eight
minor lines: Drukpa ('brugs-pa); Drikung ('bri-gung);
Taklung (sTag-lung); Trophu (Khro-phu); Yamzang (gYa'-
bzang), Shugse (Shug-seb), Mar (dMar) and Yel. In recent
centuries the fourth major branch, the Karma Kagyu, led
by the sixteen (to date) successive incarnations of H.H.
Gyalwa Karmapa (rGyal-ba Karma-pa), embodiment of the
bodhisattva Avalokiteśvara, has been the most widespread of the Kagyu schools and has now spread the fame
of the practice lineage throughout the entire world. At
this present time all disciples of Gyalwa Karmapa are
awaiting the reappearance of the *nirmāṇakāya* with fer-
vent prayers and joyous anticipation.

The origins of the Sakya tradition are more or less contemporaneous with those of the Kagyu. Its history proper begins in 1073 with the establishment by Konchog Gyalpo (dKon-mchog rGyal-po) of a *dharma* centre in Sakya, south-western Tibet, dedicated to the new *tantras*. The tradition, which thenceforth took its name from this first centre, was given definitive shape by Konchog Gyalpo's son, the 'Great Sakyapa', Kunga Nyingpo (Sachen Kun-dga' sNying-po (1092-1158)) who was heir, through his numerous teachers, to a vast range of *sūtra* and *tantra* teachings, most importantly *The Path and Its Fruit* (Lam-'bras) of the siddha Virupā.

Sachen Kunga Nyingpo was followed in the lineage by two of his sons Lopon Sonam Tsemo (sLob-dpon bSod-nams rTse-mo (1141-1182)) and Jetsun Drakpa Gyaltsen (rJe-btsun Grags-pa rGyal-mtshan (1147-1216)), both of whose accomplishments in the fields of scholarship and *tantric* meditation spread the fame of Sakya far and wide. The fourth of the great early masters of the tradition was Sakya Paṇḍita Kunga Gyaltsen Pal Zangpo (Sa-skya Pandita Kun-dga' rGyal-mtshan dPal bZang-po (1182-1251)) renowned throughout Tibet and China for his spiritual realisation and consummate mastery of both religious and secular learning. With Chogyal Phakpa (Chos-rgyal 'phags-pa (1235-1281)) nephew of Sakya Paṇḍita and last of 'the five great masters' the fame and influence of the Sakya tradition spread to Mongolia and China where Kublai Khan became his disciple. At that time the great Khan bestowed upon his guru political authority over Tibet thus initiating seventy-five years of Sakya rule.

Since numerous disciples of these five early masters taught throughout Tibet the influence of the Sakya tradition upon Buddhism in Tibet became very extensive. Many of the great masters from other schools received teachings from the holders of Sakya transmissions. Thus in the course of time the contribution made by the Sakya-pas in the fields of scholarship and meditation shaped much of the pattern of *dharma* study and practice in all schools. Foremost among later Sakya scholars and prac-titioners were such highly creative figures as Gorampa Sonam Sengge (Go-ram-pa bSod-nams Seng-ge 1428-1489) and Shakya Chogden (Shākȳa mChog-ldan 1428-1507). More recently the famed Sakya-pa master Jamyang Khentse Wangpo ('jam-dbyangs mKhyen-brtse dBang-po 1811-1892) played a leading role in spreading the rimé (ris-med — 'non-sectarian') movement which helped to bring about a renaissance of *dharma* in Tibet.

In the course of time, two principal sub-sects of the tradition have arisen. The first is the Ngor sub-sect, found-ed by the great 'Path and Fruit' master Ngorchen Kunga Zangpo (Ngor-chen Kun-dga' bZang-po 1382-1457), which had its principal centre at Ngor in Tsang province. The second sub-sect is the Tshar-pa established by the Vajrayoginī master Tsarchen Losal Gyamtso (Tsar-chen bLo-gsal rGya-mtsho 1502-1556). The headquarters of the Tshar sub-sect was Nalendrā monastery in Phenyul ('phan-yul) in Ü (dbUs) province.

The present head of the Sakya tradition is H.H. Sakya Trizin, the forty-first holder of the throne of Sakya and emanation of the *bodhisattva* Mañjuśrī. Born into the Dolma Palace branch of the Khön family in 1945, he has received .extensive teachings from such masters as Ngawang Lodro Shenphen Nyingpo, Jamyang Khyentse Chokyi Lodro and Chogay Trichen. In 1959 after the destruction of Tibetan independence, His Holiness, together with many of his followers, sought refuge in India where, at Dehra Dun in Uttar Pradesh, he has established his seat in exile. Under his wise and compas-sionate guidance the Sakya tradition has been able to maintain itself in exile.

Two
Solid Rock

THE POTENTIAL FOR achieving Buddhahood exists within every being for it is mind itself which creates both the suffering of birth and death and the bliss of enlightenment. When mind's nature is unrecognised, its clarity is mistaken for existence, the stimulus for desire, and its emptiness is misconstrued as non-existence, the stimulus for aggression. Thus the fundamental duality that underlies all experience is established. However when one comes to recognise the nature of one's own mind, delusion ceases and one is a Buddha. Since it is the practice of *dharma* and particularly the *vajrayāna* that brings about this recognition, one should begin practising without delay.

Cultivating one's potential for Buddhahood begins with 'taking refuge' in one's *guru* and the three jewels of *Buddha, dharma,* and *sangha.*

By taking refuge one is forming a connection with the fundamental truthfulness of the awakened state of mind, as represented by the objects of refuge. Henceforth one relies on them as both the ground of one's spiritual endeavours and the guiding influence in those endeavours. For these reasons, it is the ceremony of taking refuge in the presence of one's guru which defines one as a follower of *Buddha-dharma.* However the mere performance of the ceremony of taking refuge is of no benefit unless it derives from, and is sustained by,

wholesome motivation. It is said that one must go for
refuge with the threefold motivation of fear, confidence
and compassion. In this context 'fear' indicates recognition of the suffering inherent in the cycle of birth and
death. Such recognition leads one to take heart-felt refuge
in the protection of ultimate reality, unborn and unceasing, symbolised by the guru and the three jewels. Secondly, the presence of confidence in the spiritual qualities
of the guru and the three jewels as representatives of the
true nature of reality enables one to entrust oneself
without hesitation to their guidance. Finally, taking refuge
through compassion ensures that such an act will
ultimately bear fruit, not only in the benefit of oneself
but also that of all beings.

Such are the necessary ingredients in the motivation
with which one should take refuge. Now I will discuss
the objects of refuge individually, for if these are not
understood, taking refuge will obviously be meaningless.

The Guru

For those who practise the three vehicles, the guru
is the first object of refuge since it is the guru who bestows
refuge, thus introducing one to the Buddha, *dharma* and
sangha and acting henceforth as the root of spiritual pro-
gress. In the *vajrayāna*, highest of the three vehicles, the
guru is seen as the embodiment of the three jewels since
his mind is Buddha, his speech the *dharma* and his body
the *sangha*. It is the guru who awakens the qualities of
one's basic nature and informs and nurtures one's practice through the teaching of the three vehicles. For this
reason, in order to attain enlightenment, one must rely
upon a fully-qualified guru.

An authentic guru is one who has received authority from a genuine lineage and is thus able to convey the blessings of its transmission. Since this is the case, a teacher cannot be self-appointed but must have been given permission to teach by his or her own masters. As it is said in the *Fifty Verses:* 'Without the permission of your master do not perform consecrations, *maṇḍalas* or fire-offerings, do not gather disciples and do not teach'.[6] Furthermore, a *dharma*-teacher must possess the requisite qualities of learning and compassion since without these how could he lead others to liberation? For this reason again it is stated in the *Fifty Verses:* 'He should be skilled in the methods of the *mantras* and *tantras,* full of loving compassion and learned in the scriptures'.[7]

When one meets a *dharma*-teacher, with whom one feels a strong rapport, one should ignore such superficial characteristics as nationality, monastic or lay status, and style of clothing. Instead one should listen to his teachings with respect and critical intelligence. As one analyses and then puts his teachings into practice, an uncontrived sense of devotion will gradually emerge. Devotion itself signifies recognition of him as inseparable from Buddha Vajradhara since he is the one who leads us to Buddhahood through his ripening empowerments and liberating instructions. In this context such actions as offering support to one's guru and performing traditional marks of respect should be seen as both highly important and skilful practices. They act as both an expression of one's gratitude towards one's guru and openness to his teachings, and as a powerful means of further strengthening one's sense of devotion. Thus, in whatever way is appropriate to one's situation, one should try to engage in such practices, for the spiritual merit that is gained through assisting one's guru with a devoted mind is immensely beneficial.

For further details on this vital point of the relationship between the guru and student, one should ask one's

guru for the transmission of such teachings as Tsarchen
Losal Gyamtso's commentary on the *Fifty Verses,* Za
Patrul's *'Instructions of Guru Samantabhadra'* or Gampopa's *Ornament of Liberation*.[8] In all of these the
necessity of studying with a guru, such a teacher's
qualifications, and the attitude and actions incumbent
upon the disciple are clearly explained.

Buddha

The jewel of Buddha is the first of the three jewels
since it is Buddha who revealed the jewel of the true
dharma, or teachings, which have been practised by the
jewel of *sangha.*

Referring to Buddha's primacy among the three
jewels, Maitreya declared in the *'Ultimate Continuum
Treatise':* 'In the ultimate sense only the Buddha is the
refuge of beings, because the conqueror possesses the
body of the *dharma* and this is the ultimate attainment
of the *sangha*.'[9]

A Buddha, as exemplified by the historical Buddha
Śākyamuni, is a being who, having purified the two
obscurations of emotional defilements and nescience,
awakens to the actual nature of all phenomena. Such an
enlightened one possesses two modes of being: the *dharmakāya* (body of truth) and *rūpakāya* (body of form).
The *dharmakāya* is the underlying nature of all Buddhas
since it signifies the state of identity with the true nature
of reality which every Buddha has attained. The *dharmakāya* itself is free from production or cessation and,
being totally unelaborated, one cannot assert either its
existence or its non-existence. Since the *dharmakāya* is
thus inaccessible to the dualistic thought patterns of
unenlightened beings, the Buddha communicates in the

consensually created realm within which ordinary beings operate by manifesting the *rūpakāya*. The manner in which the Buddha manifests the *rūpakāya*, the effortless expression of His intrinsic compassion, can be likened to the way in which the moon, while remaining in the sky, is reflected in countless pools of water upon the earth. Furthermore the *rūpakāya* itself posssesses two modes of appearance in relation to the two different levels on which beings are to be trained. Thus, in the visionary realm of cosmic splendour and significance attained by highly advanced *bodhisattvas*, the Buddha displays the *sambhogakāya* (enjoyment body) form endowed with the five certainties of teacher, time, place, audience, and teaching. However, in the realm of mundane experience in which ordinary beings dwell, the Buddha manifests a variety of *nirmāṇakāya* ('emanation body') forms to present the *dharma*. These *nirmāṇakāya* forms are divided into three distinct types: *nirmāṇakāya* of birth, which the Buddha manifests in such roles as that of a king in order to benefit beings; *nirmāṇakāya* of skill whereby He trains beings through such devices as artistic performance; and supreme *nirmāṇakāya* through which Buddha reveals Himself openly as Buddha and accomplishes twelve great deeds [10] to lead beings to enlightenment.

Taking refuge in the Buddha who embodies these qualities and modes of being, is of tremendous importance. The jewel of Buddha represents the fulfillment of one's own innate potential for Buddhahood. Thus, through taking refuge in this jewel, one has formed a direct connection to the reality of enlightenment.

Dharma

The path to Buddhahood is to be discovered through the practice of the jewel of *dharma*. In essence, the *dharma* comprises two aspects: direct realisation and scriptural tradition. 'Direct realisation' is the meditative insight into the true nature of reality which leads one to enlightenment. Although this realisation itself is thus the crucial occurrence in one's spiritual life, it depends upon the systematic study and practice of the teachings contained in the scriptural tradition, for these provide the foundation from which such direct insight springs.

This second aspect of the jewel of *dharma*, the scriptural tradition, is the record of Buddha's word collected in the three 'baskets' of *sūtra, abhidharma,*[11] and *vinaya.*[12] These teachings were given by Lord Buddha in three distinct periods in each of which He presented the doctrine at a different level and from a different perspective. In the first period, or 'first turning of the wheel of *dharma*' Lord Buddha explained the doctrines of the *hīnayāna* such as the four noble truths of suffering and its cause, cessation and its cause. In the second period He discoursed on the Perfection of Wisdom of the *mahāyāna* and in the third, or final, period, He gave teachings on the 'mind-only' view and buddha-nature.

In addition to these *sūtra* teachings the word of Lord Buddha includes the *'mantra'* teachings of *vajrayāna*. The very powerful and subtle instructions of the *vajrayāna* were delivered privately by Lord Buddha to particularly advanced disciples. They were subsequently transmitted to succeeding generations of practitioners in great secrecy until they became well-known and widespread amongst *dharma*-practitioners in India and Tibet at a much later time. The jewel of *dharma* thus provides a totality of paths to enlightenment based on meditative experience and the collection of instructions which inspire it. Through taking refuge in this jewel, one obtains the key to the highway to Buddhahood.

Sangha

Since Lord Buddha has announced the path to enlightenment and since the *dharma* is that path, the members of the *sangha*, or spiritual community, are the ones who help us to travel the path. The *sangha* in which one takes refuge consists of both spiritually-advanced beings and ordinary practitioners who have entered the *dharma* prior to us. The *arhats* [13] and *bodhisattvas*[14] who comprise the advanced or 'noble' *sangha* include such figures as the monk-disciples of Lord Buddha, Śāriputra and Mahāmaudgalyayana who obtained arhat-ship, and 'lay' *bodhisattvas* such as Mañjuśrī and Avalokiteśvara who have scaled the *mahāyāna* spiritual levels.[15] Their example of perfect conduct and the power of their meditation remain as a source of blessings for subsequent generations of practitioners.

The *sangha* of so-called ordinary practitioners comprises practitioners of each of the three vehicles. Thus the *sangha* of the *hīnayāna* are those who uphold the *prātimokṣa* (individual liberation) vows, be they laymen or women maintaining the five precepts or monks maintaining two hundred and fifty precepts. Those who in addition to this also maintain the *bodhisattva* vow to achieve Buddhahood for the benefit of all beings, are known as the *mahāyāna sangha*, and those who in addition to maintaining both the *prātimokṣa* and *bodhisattva* vows also uphold the *vidyadhara*[16] vows received at the time of *tantric* empowerment, are known as the *vajrayāna sangha*.

When one takes refuge in the *sangha* one is entering into a community of fellowship which has at its heart the path to Buddhahood. One's own commitment to spiritual development is thus anchored firmly in the wider environment of collective practice, and the limitations and difficulties which arise if one practises as if one were an isolated individual are overcome.

Although the guru, buddha, *dharma* and *sangha* are seen as the objects of refuge, from the specific standpoint of *vajrayāna* practice each of the three jewels has corresponding *vajrayāna* objects of refuge known collectively as 'the three roots'. Thus the corresponding *vajrayāna* aspect of Buddha is the guru who is the 'root' of the blessings that ripen one's mind, the essential function of an enlightened teacher. The corresponding *vajrayāna* aspect of he *dharma* is the *yidam* (yi-dam, 'meditation-deity'), root of spiritual attainment *(siddhis)* since these are the fruit of *yidam* meditation. Finally, the corresponding *vajrayāna* aspect of the *sangha* is represented by the *dākinīs* (mkha'-'gro-ma/lit. 'sky-goers'), the feminine spiritual embodiments of awakened energy manifesting in life-situations as the root of enlightened activity.

After taking refuge one should ask one's guru to bestow the *prātimokṣa* (individual liberation) vows which represent the discipline of the *hīnayāna*. For monks and nuns this discipline comprises numerous vows but for lay-practitioners it comprises five precepts which are to abstain from: 'taking life, taking what is not given, sexual misconduct, false and harmful speech and intoxication. Such moral behaviour creates the space in which meditation and study can develop free from the compulsive habits of self-privileging and indulgence. Furthermore, because these precepts restrain one from harming others they act as a catalyst for the dawn of selfless compassion which is expressed in the discipline of the second vehicle, *the mahāyāna*. In summary, with refuge and this ensuing adoption of moral discipline, one has become established on a spiritual ground of solid rock and has thus become ready to receive and utilise the instructions of the three vehicles which will take one directly to enlightenment.

Three

Tasting birth
and death

HAVING TAKEN REFUGE one must now experience the simplicity of renunciation through the four contemplations: precious human birth, impermanence, action and the defects of *saṃsāra* ('cyclical existence'), which may be termed the basic teaching of the first of the three vehicles, the *hīnayāna*. One's subsequent entry into the profound meditations of the *mahāyāna* and *vajrayāna* is predicated on these fundamental teachings of Lord Buddha since they lay bare the workings of the defiled mind which entangles us in *saṃsāra* through the poisons of desire, aggression and delusion. Through these four reflections one comes to taste the undiluted reality of birth and death as it is and, when this happens, an unfeigned renunciation of *saṃsāra* will arise.

Precious Human Birth

The possession of human birth provides the working basis for liberation. All sentient beings possess the potential for Buddhahood but only those who have obtained human birth are in a position to bring this potential to fruition. However although it is so beneficial, human birth occurs only rarely in the cycle of birth and death. Its chief cause is prior virtuous, one might say 'humane' behaviour. Since truly virtuous actions are rare, human birth comes about relatively infrequently. Indeed, in comparison with other forms of sentient life in this infinite universe, it is numerically infinitesimal. As is says in *Entering the Bodhisattva Conduct:*

'The Lord therefore said that it is as difficult to obtain human birth as it is for a tortoise's neck to enter a hole in a yoke floating on the ocean.'[17]

The reason why human birth acts as the uniquely suitable basis for attaining Buddhahood is that it embodies both freedom from entrapment in eight limiting states and the possession of ten factors that facilitate the relationship with the *dharma* necessary for enlightenment. These eight negative situations that preclude the possibility of engaging in religious practice are:

(i) birth as a hell being (ii) animal (iii) long-living god, (iv) ghost, (v) fool, (vi) barbarian, (vii) possessing wrong views, (viii) living at a time when no Buddha has appeared.

The positive conditions are:

(i) being born as a human being, (ii) living in a land where religion is practised, (iii) possessing sound senses, (iv) possessing faith in religion, (v) having refrained from committing heinous actions, (vi) a Buddha has appeared, (vii) a Buddha has taught the doctrine, (viii) the doctrine still exists, (ix) the doctrine has genuine followers, (x) one has compassion for others.

Having obtained such a precious human birth, it is an act of folly to squander it. As it says in the *Friendly Letter*: 'Having obtained a human birth, one who commits sins is more foolish than one who fills a jewel-adorned golden vessel with vomit'.[18]

Impermanence and Death

At this stage in one's contemplation, one's sense of the preciousness of this life should be deepened by the recognition of impermanence. Since there is not one person in history who has escaped death, how can one expect to be exempted? As it says in *Entering the Bodhisattva Conduct:* 'Why should it not be that death should befall such a one as me'?[19] Inevitability is evident in the decay and collapse which are woven into the very fabric of the universe. Life, based as it is on the temporary union of body and mind, is part of that fabric. As it is said in the *Thirty-Seven Practices of a Buddha's Child:* 'The mind's just a guest in the hotel of the body. One day it must depart and travel beyond'.[20] Furthermore, one would be deluding oneself if one were to acknowledge the inevitability of death but nevertheless imagine that its coming were fixed at some point in the comfortably-distant future. Actually, the time of death is very uncertain. As it is said:

> 'Some die while in the womb
> So too, some die on just being born,
> So, too, some die while just crawling
> So, too, while able to run about
> Some old and some young
> Some while in the prime of life'.[21]

In every period of life there are a multiplicity of dangers, and, by contrast, comparatively few life-enhancing elements. Indeed, even life-supporting systems like food and medical treatment can be fatal. Thus the reality of death is always with us. At the moment of death, mind and body separate and go their own different ways. Those things upon which we have placed so much reliance: friends, wealth and power will not help us. Only prior practice of the *dharma* will be of any use to us.

Action

The whole range of life-situations that comprise *saṃsāra* have their roots in our actions. No external power, nor random chance, has contrived our present position in the cycle of birth and death. The imprints of our actions — physical, verbal and mental — are deposited in the continuum of our mind and ripen, when the appropriate conditions obtain, as the various sufferings and joys of life in the six realms. Since mind itself, being non-physical, cannot be destroyed and therefore continues to be embodied until liberation, there is no limit to the ripening of deeds.

To contemplate action, one should begin by considering non-virtuous actions and their results. Non-virtuous actions are ten in number:

> taking the life of a sentient being, whether it be insect or human, embryo or adult[22]
> taking what is not given
> sexual misconduct
> lying
> slander
> harsh speech
> frivolous speech
> covetousness
> malevolence
> perverse views

These sinful actions mature as sufferings in various ways. In general it can be said that deeds motivated by aggression lead to birth in the hell realm, those motivated by greed to birth in the ghost realm, and those motivated by ignorance to birth in the animal realm. Moreover, the fruit of deeds can ripen in experiences similar to the causes, an example of which would be the way in which killing can generate a vulnerability to early death. The force of actions can also mature in the establishment of habits, instanced by the brutalisation that can develop once the act of killing has occurred. One's actions alter one's physical and social environment and an example of this process would be the creation, by killing, of an environment in which the necessities for supporting life were scarce.

The ten virtuous actions may simply be described as the abandoning of sinful deeds. Thus, for example, the renunciation of killing constitutes the primary virtuous deed. Just as negative actions produce the miseries of *saṃsāra*, so all the joyful experiences one encounters in the six realms originate in one's virtuous deeds. Since this is so, one should delight in such actions. As Nāgārjuna has stated: 'Morality is said to be the foundation of all qualities, just as the earth is the support of both animate and inanimate things'.[23]

Defects of Saṃsāra

The fourth and final reflection is the reflection on wordly existence and its suffering. This suffering displays itself in three modes: the suffering of suffering, the suffering of change, and the suffering of conditionality.

The suffering of suffering constitutes the temporary entrapment in the three lower realms of animal, ghost

and hell being. Jetsun Drakpa Gyaltsen says: 'The suffering of suffering is the misery of the three lower
realms'.[24] The cause of existence in these lower realms
of misery lies within our own mind. If, at the time of
death, aggression is dominant in our mental continuum,
the imprint of this defilement will cause rebirth into a
variety of projected hellish environments. Likewise,
rebirth into the ghost realm is structured through the
imprint of avarice. Due to such obsession, in this realm
one experiences a series of hallucinatory episodes of
deprivation.

Finally, rebirth in the animal realm comes about
through the defilement of ignorance: the habitual disuse
of one's capacity for reflection and choice, themselves the
seeds of virtuous action. Here as is often sadly evident,
animals endure a life of being preyed upon and of prey-
ing upon their fellows, of helpless slavery and exploitation.

The suffering of change is displayed by the way in
which every situation that appears to promise lasting happiness, success, wealth or power, inevitably reveals itself
as suffering in a new guise. When considering the human
state, one cannot deny that despite fleeting moments of
bliss, one is bound by the four awesome rivers of birth,
old-age, sickness and death. Furthermore, in human life,
one is also afflicted by the desire for what one cannot
have, difficulty in maintaining what one has, the pain of
separation from one's dear ones, and association with
hateful people.

Both the demi-god *(asura)* and god realms are
irredeemably flawed. Thus the pleasures of the god realm,
deriving as they do from a mixture of virtue and pride,
seem to represent a perpetual reward but their built-in
flaw is their very transitoriness. In addition, in the case
of those reborn in the realm of the demi-gods a further
suffering inherent in their experience is their conti-

nuing struggle for spiritual power or status, a struggle deriving from jealousy. Thus one should not be seduced by the limited aim of gaining the pleasures of the higher realms, whether as a human or divine being. These environments, however seemingly wondrous, are no refuge from *saṃsāra*, simply just another facet of it.

The suffering of conditionality is the most fundamental of sufferings for it inheres in one's mistaken notion that the five psycho-physical constituents of form, feeling, perception, formations and consciousness constitute an autonomous, permanent self. This delusion acts as a magnet, attracting to itself all miseries from life to life. However ordinary beings do not recognise this fabrication of a self out of the constituents as suffering, but instead believe it to be the source of happiness. Only those who possess the eye of insight see this suffering of conditionality for what it is:

> 'A single hair on the palm of the hand
> If it enters the eye
> Causes unpleasantness and pain.
> The fools who resemble the palm of the hand
> Do not feel the hair, the suffering of conditionality,
> But saintly people, who are like the eye
> Experience it as misery.'[25]

As one familiarises oneself with the reality of *saṃsāra* the conviction should arise that there is no security or bliss to be found here. Once one becomes imbued with this sense, a longing for liberation will arise. Such longing itself generates an unshakeable commitment to *dharma*-practice, since it is only through this that such liberation can be won. As Gampopa declares:

> 'By contemplating the difficulty of obtaining leisure

and opportunity you will be incited to *dharma*.

By contemplating death and impermanence you will be incited to virtue.

By contemplating the inevitable cause and effect of actions you will be incited to abandon sin.

By contemplating the defects of *saṃsāra* you will be incited to accomplish liberation'.[26]

Four

Open Heart

CONTEMPLATION OF THE 'four thoughts' endows our practice with the seriousness of renunciation. However, this renunciation alone is not sufficient to lead us to Buddhahood. Since one does not exist as a totally discrete or solitary being in *saṃsāra*, the resolve to untie oneself alone from this net of suffering must be extended outwards in the *bodhicitta* ('thought of enlightenment'), the altruistic resolve to attain Buddhahood for the benefit of all beings. As it says in *Parting From the Four Attachments:* 'There is no benefit in liberating oneself alone, for the beings of the three realms are my fathers and mothers. To leave my parents in the midst of distress, while desiring happiness, would be evil-hearted.'[27] With this thought one enters into the practice of the second of the three vehicles, the *mahāyāna.*

Liberation itself is impossible without *bodhicitta*. The habitual unawareness which entraps us within *saṃsāra* can only be transcended through the alchemy of *bodhicitta*, awakened thought, which transforms the attitudes of self-cherishing and self-clinging, the roots of *saṃsāra*, into all-embracing compassion. Once this alchemy is at work it provides the continuing impetus to Buddhahood. As it is said in *Entering the Bodhisattva Conduct:*

'It is like the supreme gold-making elixir

For it transforms the unclean body we have taken
Into the precious jewel of a Buddha-form
Therefore firmly seize the *bodhicitta*'.[28]

Bodhicitta manifests in both conventional and
ultimate aspects. In the realm of conventional truth, that
is to say the consensually-created world inhabited by sentient beings in the illusion-like cycle of birth and death,
one develops *bodhicitta* as great compassion impelling one
to Buddhahood for the benefit of those beings. This
resolution itself is embodied in the ceremony of the
bodhisattva vow through which one truly enters into the
mahāyāna. Secondly, on the basis of this *bodhicitta*, one
comes to enter into direct apprehension of the state of
reality as it is, free even from the notions of subject,
object, and act of compassion, since such concepts are
still dualistic and hence ultimately invalid. Such non-dual
insight is ultimate *bodhicitta*.

Loving-Kindness

Open-hearted *bodhicitta* arises in dependence upon
the supports of loving-kindness and compassion which,
in turn, arise in dependence upon the recognition of all
beings as our kin: 'limbs of one life'. When one actually
investigates *saṃsāra* one cannot find any beginning to
it since every effect depends upon prior causes and conditions. As this is so, it is reasonable to conclude that all
beings must have been directly related to one another
innumerable times. Thus one is led to acknowledge all
beings as one's previous mothers and fathers.

Once this ground has been established one can pro-
ceed to practice loving-kindness meditation, taking one's
own mother as the initial object of meditation. Recalling

her incalculable kindness one is led to admit one's indebtedness to her which can only be repaid through generating total love to her, thus pervading her with the wish that she obtain happiness and the cause of happiness, which is virtue. As this meditative intention towards one's mother becomes resolute, one should extend it gradually towards one's relatives, friends, enemies, and eventually to the whole of the six realms in the recognition that each and every being has been one's mother and is therefore connected with one just as intimately as the mother of this life. In this way, the strength of love towards our present mother is expanded to encompass all beings.

Compassion

Once loving-kindness has become a stable feature in our outlook and our interaction with the world it should be deepened into compassion. Compassion, in essence, is the wish that all beings be liberated from suffering and its causes, which are sinful actions. The stages of meditative intention are identical with those of love, beginning with our present mother and reaching completion in the pervasion of all beings with a steady, undiminishing intention. One point which should be emphasised concerns the attachment that people generally feel towards loved ones. If one utilises this attachment skilfully, it will not be an obstacle but an aid to the development of open-heartedness. One's love for one's children or parents, for instance, works in this meditation like a magnet to attract to itself all other beings, since they too are our parents and children, albeit from other times and other places. It would be a sad error to imagine that, before embracing all beings with tenderness, one had first to coldly reject those who are at this time our closest companions and dependents. How could universal love grow from such stony ground?

Bodhicitta

Acknowledging our kinship with others creates a vivid and penetrating sense of their suffering. How can our wish that they might come to have happiness and be free from sorrow be achieved when at this very moment they are floundering in an ocean of misery? In one's present state as an unenlightened being, one does not have the capability to free them from *saṃsāra*. Only Buddha, possessing a wisdom that comprehends the nature of phenomena, a compassion that embraces all beings without partiality, and an energy that is inexhaustible, is able to do this. Since this is the case one must respond to beings' sufferings by resolving to obtain Buddhahood, the very fulfillment of one's Buddha-nature. Through such resolution, *bodhicitta* is born.

Bodhicitta arises in two phases, that of aspiration and that of application. As it is said in *Entering the Bodhisattva Conduct:* 'In brief, *bodhicitta* should be understood to be of two types: aspiration thought and application thought. As is understood by the distinction between aspiring to go and going, so the wise understand in turn the distinction between these two'.[29] Thus, in aspirational *bodhicitta* one generates the actual intention to achieve Buddhahood, and this naturally extends into the application of this intention when one commits oneself to practising the actual stages of the path to Buddhahood. In the words of *Entering the Bodhisattva Conduct:* 'Just as the previous Blessed Ones gave birth to *bodhicitta*, and just as they successively dwelt in the *bodhisattva* practices, likewise for the sake of all beings, I give birth to *bodhicitta* and likewise shall too successively follow the practices'.[30]

An habitual self-cherishing, self-privileging attitude is the enemy of open-heartedness. One cannot accomplish the *bodhicitta* of application with a heart that is filled with one's own interest. To excise self-cherishing, which has encrusted one's innate potential for compassion, one should practise the two *bodhicitta* meditations known as 'equalising oneself with others' and 'exchanging oneself for others'. As it is said in *Entering the Bodhisattva Conduct:* 'First of all I should strive to meditate upon the equality of myself and others. I should protect all beings as I do myself since we are all equal in wanting pleasure and not wanting pain'.[31] Self-cherishing dissolves in this simple yet over-powering recognition where there is no great or small, young or old and where all beings are perceived as 'wishfulfilling gems'.

With this surrender of one's claim to 'specialness', one can afford to open completely to others in the second *bodhicitta* meditation: exchanging oneself for others. This practice is known as 'the secret teaching of the *mahāyanā*. As it says in *Entering the Bodhisattva Conduct:* 'Those who quickly wish to afford protection to themselves and others should practise the supreme mystery of exchanging oneself for others'.[32] As we have seen, it is self-cherishing which blocks the flourishing of compassion in one's life, yet if one stops to examine this 'self' to which one is so attached, one can easily see that it is a mere conceptual imputation upon the sperm, ovum and attaching consciousness that have come together at the moment of conception. Until this day, one has naively projected the notion of self, an autonomous, unchanging identity, upon this dependently-arisen phenomenon. However, this might just as validly be projected upon any such aggregation of sperm, ovum and consciousness since, as an aggregation, this entity is actually devoid of the supposed characteristics of self-hood.

Armed with this liberating deconstruction of self-cherishing one is now empowered to utilise the fiction of self-identity in the immensely skilful technique of exchanging self for others. In meditative contemplation and in everyday life one should transfer the notion of self on to others and thus take others as being oneself, object of all one's care and cherishing. One thus reverses habitual perception and sees oneself as others, in other words: as an other, a stranger. With this reorientation of one's interpretative structures, one automatically cherishes others with the same intimacy and intensity which one had previously lavished upon oneself since they have now become that very self. Emotions such as envy and pride which arise in the wake of self-cherishing are also integrated into, and liberated in, this practice since they too are now directed towards the benefit of one's 'new self': that is to say, other beings. As it says in *Entering the Bodhisattva Conduct:* 'Considering lesser beings and so forth as myself and considering myself as the other, I should meditate upon envy, competitiveness and pride with a mind freed from concepts'.[33] Through this exchange of self for others, the hopes, fears and misery of other beings become one's own. The remaining walls of self's privacy collapse because of the full acceptance of others' suffering onto oneself and the output of one's own happiness and virtue onto them. Such is the sacred heart of *bodhicitta*. 'May all the sufferings of the three realms ripen in myself. By the blessing of this virtue may all sentient beings attain Buddhahood'.[34]

A particularly effective way of meditating on this exchange is to link the taking of others' sufferings and the sending of one's happiness to the inhalation and exhalation of breath. When one breathes in, one should imagine that the sufferings and sins of beings are inhaled into oneself in the form of black smoke. Subsequently on exhalation, one should visualise that one is sending one's virtues and happiness to all beings in the form of moon-rays or sun-rays. Since this 'sending and taking' technique is rooted in the very rhythms of our life, as expressed in breath, it possesses great power.[35]

Five

The Crystal Key

THE UNCONDITIONAL COMPASSION of *bodhicitta* establishes the space in which clear vision can arise. Such clear vision into the very nature of phenomena is termed 'ultimate *bodhicitta*'. However although the altruistic *bodhicitta* of conventional truth is the ground of this vision, ultimate *bodhicitta* itself generally requires the specific step-by-step development of calm abiding (zhi-gnas) and insight (lhag-mthong). It is in fact insight which constitutes *bodhicitta's* clear vision, since it is insight which decisively cuts through the knots of self-clinging by revealing the true nature of mind. However, without the prior development of calm-abiding, insight would be mere conceptual posturing. As it says in *Entering the Bodhisattva Conduct:* 'Having understood that defilements are completely overcome by insight endowed with calm-abiding, first of all I should seek calm-abiding.[36]

Calm-Abiding Meditation

The essence of calm-abiding meditation is oneness of mind in which habitual dichotomising chatter and neurotic tensions come to rest in stillness. As it says in the *Jewel-Cloud sūtra:* 'What is calm-abiding? It is one-pointedness of mind'.[37] When calm-abiding arises one simply rests in the vivid clarity of mind that has

manifested with the evaporation of the clouds of conceptualisation. However, for most people, such uncontrived
calmness does not develop automatically. For this reason
it is useful to train in the various skilful means of stabilis-
ing the mind until obstructions fall away and this
effortless calmness reveals itself. Prior even to practising the various stages of settling the mind, it is very
helpful to have some knowledge of the five major pit-
falls to practice, which are: Laziness and forgetfulness of
instructions, 'sinking' with dullness or 'scattering' with
inattentiveness, non-application of remedial factors when
necessary in one's meditation, and over-application of
such remedies when they are no longer needed. Equipped with a knowledge of such obstacles and the ability
to apply antidotes such as faith, energy, aspiration, relax-
ation, mindfulness and clear-comprehension, one will be
able to gain success in meditation.

The actual stages of settling the mind until it rests
naturally in calmness are nine in number:

> *Settling.* Having adopted the correct
> meditation-posture one should focus on a
> suitable object of concentration such as a
> Buddha-image, a blue flower, a blue silken cloth,
> or a syllable such as the letter A, positioned
> directly before one.
> *Continual Settling.* Since beginners cannot con-
> centrate for long periods it is most suitable to
> practice in short but frequent sessions.
> *Re-settling.* When attention wanders, one
> should remain undiscouraged and simply re-
> direct the mind to the object.
> *Perfect Settling.* Employing mindfulness one
> should place the mind completely on the object.
> *Subduing.* If 'sinking' arises at this stage, one

should 'tighten' the mind by lifting one's gaze and focussing upon the clear sky. If 'scattering' is the problem one should instil a sense of 'groundedness' by lowering one's gaze or meditating in a darkened room.

Pacifying. If distraction creates a feeling of unease in one's meditation or if a wish to discontinue arises, one should stabilise the mind by holding it strongly on the object.

Perfectly Pacifying. Likewise, if the very powerful opponents of meditation such as covetousness or malevolence develop, one pacifies the mind by strong settling.

One-pointedness. When wandering thought still occurs preventing full achievement of calmness, one should settle the mind directly on the thoughts themselves, thus integrating them into one's meditation.

Even settling. Through the practice of the preceding stages, the mind will eventually come to rest effortlessly in itself. When this happens the skilful device of focussing upon an object is no longer necessary. One's meditation becomes relaxed and simple and one's mind is both flexible and clear. One is now ready to enter into insight meditation.

Insight Meditation

Insight meditation through which the ultimately selfless nature of all phenomena is discerned, constitutes the practice of the perfection of wisdom. It is this wisdom which transforms all practice into the path. Without wisdom the other five perfections of the *mahāyāna:* giving, morality, patience, energy and meditation will not lead one to Buddhahood. Thus it says in *Entering the Middle Way:* 'Just as a group of blind men are easily led by a single man who can see the desired place, so here also, taking the qualities with the eye of intellect one goes to the state of the victors'.[38] In the *hīnayāna*, insight only uproots the deluded notion of self as it applies to the personality. However, here in the *mahāyāna* it also cuts through the delusion of selfhood in any phenomenon whatsoever, thus laying bare the essential emptiness of reality. This realisation may be termed 'mother of all Buddhas'. As it says in *Entering the Middle Way:* 'Nonself is for the liberation of beings. Phenomena and the self are said to be the two types (of non-self). Therefore the teacher taught the disciples according to these divisions'.[39]

When commencing insight meditation, one should allow one's mind to settle — limpid yet clear. In this state of stillness one should analyse the idea of a personal self: an autonomous, discrete, unchanging and controlling identity. Is this self identical with one's body, one's name or one's mind? To assert that the body is the location of the self is contradictory since the body, being a compound and impermanent phenomenon cannot fulfill the functional requirements of an autonomous self. Likewise, to assert that one's name constitutes the self is an error since name, being merely a linguistic convention, utterly lacks the characteristics of autonomy and unchangingness. Furthermore, one's mind is continually changing and cannot therefore be postulated as a locus of the self. Even if one were to insist that a new mental self was established at each successive moment, one would still be mistaken since the very notion of a present moment involving as it necessarily must, the three phases of beginning, middle and end, is infinitely divisible. One can therefore never reach a definitive 'present moment' and the notion of a 'self' predicated on the basis of such a moment is untenable. It is now possible to understand that the personal self which is imputed on the name, body or mind, exists only in the way in which a snake exists when a coloured rope is misperceived by a short-sighted man.

At this point in one's meditation, one might imagine, as the *hīnayānists* do, that although there is no personal self, reality is comprised of an ever-changing field of momentary, yet inherently existent, phenomena. Although such a view is superior to those of non-Buddhists, it is mistaken from the point of view of ultimate truth. As it says in *Entering the Bodhisattva Conduct:* 'Furthermore among the yogins, there are differences in understanding. Those with higher views contradict those with lower views'.[40] Continuing in meditation, one should therefore thoroughly examine all phenomena until one recognises that the basis of all appearances is simply mind. As Lord Buddha declared in the *Ten Earths Sūtra*: 'The three realms are just mind, sons of the Conqueror'.[41] Those phenomena which one assumes to have an independent external existence have, in reality, been established by mind; rather like dream appearances which although fascinating or fearsome at the time are subsequently recognised as lacking inherent existence. One should examine all the various manifestations of this projection in one's own experience. Even the notion of an ultimately irreducible building block such as the atom is found, when analysed, to be devoid of inherent existence and to have been established in dependence on mind. If one considers this, one will realise that such an entity, in order to be able to constitute with other entities the basis of the world, would have to possess internal and external dimensions. Since this is so, the notion of a partless and therefore irreducible entity is impossible. Such an entity can only exist as a projection of mind.

One should also subject mundane objects such as water, food, faces and bodies to similar scrutiny. In each case one will conclude that each phenomenon has been established through the power of imprints or tendencies that bias or condition the mind. Even excrement which is a repulsive substance to most humans, is delicious food to flies. Similarly poisonous substances or disease microbes cannot ultimately be established as such since they too may be beneficial to certain subjects.

To conclude at this point that external phenomena are indeed created by mind but that this mind, the perceiving subject, is ultimately existent, is to go further astray. If the object, the external world, cannot be established as inherently existent equally and obviously the subject, the perceiving consciousness, cannot be established as such either. Without an object, how can there be a subject? Both subject and object are mutually dependent projections of mind itself. As Vasubandhu says: 'Because the object does not exist, there is no subject'.[42] Such an understanding is very profound but does not constitute complete insight. One should thus persevere in meditation until the view is perfected in the *Madhyamaka*.

Look at mind itself in meditation. Like a crystal it reflects all the appearances of the phenomenal world, yet one cannot find any identifiable essence to it. Examine it for its colour: Is it yellow, blue, red, or green? Its shape: Is it oblong, square, circular or triangular? Its location: Is it inside or outside the body or somewhere inbetween? From whence does it originate? Where does it endure right now, and where will it go? In each case one will realise that upon analysis no identifiable essence can be found. It is empty of colour, shape or location. It has no point of origination, destination, and no duration in the present moment. The more one searches for essence, the more elusive this becomes.

Yet if one were now to conclude that mind, like the child of a barren woman, is simply non-existent one would be falling into the deluded extremist view of nihilism by mistaking mind's essential emptiness for mere non-existence. For mind, although it cannot be discovered anywhere, is the very basis for the manifestation of the phenomenal world. Thus, while it cannot be termed existent since it is devoid of the attributes of existence, it cannot be non-existent either. In this way mind is beyond the conceptual elaboration of the two extremes, the inevitably deluded projections of dualistic mind. Such projections entirely disappear with this recognition, like fears imagined in darkness seen later in the light of day.

Six

The Path of
the Emperor

ONCE *BODHICITTA* HAS arisen in the space of open-heartedness, one should enter into the third vehicle, the *vajrayāna*. It is the practice of this vehicle, expounded in the *tantras* by Lord Buddha, which alone will enable one to achieve Buddhahood for the benefit of all sentient beings in this very life. If one questions why this is so, the answer lies in the superiority of its skilful methods for achieving realisation. These in turn rely upon the reality of mind's nature, which being the union of luminosity and emptiness, is actually primordial wisdom. Since this wisdom exists in all sentient beings, though currently unrecognised, the goal of buddhahood is not to be found external to our mind. It is this continuum *(tantra)* of the wisdom-nature of mind shared by both deluded sentient beings and enlightened Buddhas, which gives its name to the teachings *(tantras)* presented by Lord Buddha in the *vajrayāna*. As it says in *'The General System of Tantra Sets'*: *'Tantra* means one's mind being non-dual primordial wisdom. It is an unbroken continuum from beginningless time until Buddhahood'.[43]

However, although understanding this true nature of mind is the ground of *vajrayāna* practice, it cannot be understood through scriptural tradition and reasoning alone but depends upon the receipt of the blessing of one's guru. As Jamgon Kongtrul Lodro Thaye states: 'When the blessings of the glorious guru and one's *karma* come together one realises one's nature like meeting an old friend'.[44] Since this is the case, one must exert oneself in the meditation of *guru-yoga* through which one realises the blessings of one's guru for as Ngawang Legpa states: 'It is said that in order to behold the natural face of the profound true nature of all phenomena there is nothing superior to *guru-yoga*'.[45]

Infused with the guru's blessings, when one settles once more in meditation upon mind's nature one comes to recognise that whilst mind is beyond all conceptual elaborations the unceasing flow of manifestations that one terms *saṃsāra* and *nirvāṇa* appear as the expression of its luminous or 'clear-light' quality. Yet this luminosity, when examined, is found to be devoid of origination, duration or cessation, being utterly empty of intrinsic nature or inherent existence through which it could be apprehended. Mind is thus simultaneously luminous and empty. As *saṃsāra* and *nirvāṇa* are themselves merely expressions of this mind, one need not attempt to abandon *saṃsāra* and obtain in its stead *nirvāṇa*. As is said in the *Hevajra Tantra:* 'By rejecting *saṃsāra* one will not obtain *nirvāṇa*,'[46] and as Lord Marpa declares: 'Do not desire to abandon *saṃsāra*. There is no *nirvāṇa* to attain. *Saṃsāra* and *nirvāṇa* are the self-liberated innate state. Realise their unity as great bliss'.[47] One should therefore settle decisively in this view of the inseparability of *saṃsāra* and *nirvāṇa*. In such a state the *vajrayāna* meditator need not reject the objects of the senses unlike the ordinary practitioner who considers these to be poisons, inimical to liberation. Indeed with the *vajrayāna* view of innate purity sense objects are transformed into aids to the spiritual path. As it says in *'The General System of the Tantra Sets':* 'If one questions whether one will not be bound by objects, the answer is that ordinary beings who do not possess skilful means will be bound by them but for those who do possess skilful means, they will become aids to liberation'.[48]

Whilst scholars of the ancient *tantra* tradition delineate six tantra sets: *kriyā, upa, yoga, mahā-yoga, anu-yoga,* and *ati-yoga,* great scholars of the new *tantra* schools such as Lobpon Sonam Tsemo refer to only four sets: *kriyā, cārya, yoga* and *anuttara.* The *kriyā tantras* are designed primarily for those practitioners who are attracted to external spiritual activities such as purification rituals. The *cārya tantras* are for those who wish to practise a mixture of external activities and internal meditation, whilst the *yoga-tantras* embody primarily internal meditation. The highest set of *tantras,* the *anuttara tantras* are for those who wish to practise the supremely skilful methods of the development and fulfilment stage. Furthermore, this last set is divided into three sub-sets: 'Father *tantras'* such as Guhyasāma-ja, 'mother' *tantras* such as Cakrasamvara and non-dual *tantras* such as Śrī Hevajra, King of *tantras.*

In each of the *tantra* sets one practises deity (yi-dam) yoga through visualisation, recitation and gesture. One practises in this way because the perception of oneself and one's environment as pure, sacred appearance is the fundamental characteristic of the *vajrayāna* path, grounded as it is in the view of all appearances as the manifestation of the luminosity and emptiness of mind. Furthermore, it is deity meditation which functions as the supreme antidote to the conceptualisation of self. As is said in the 'Path and Its Fruit': 'Just as a stable poison is an antidote for a moving poison so deity conceptualisa-tion is the antidote for ordinary conceptualisation.'[49] However, although the meditations on the three lower *tantras* such as the meditations on the 'Lords of the Three Families': Avalokiteśvara, Mañjuśrī and Vajrapāṇi are very beneficial, it is only the *anuttaratantra* that leads to the attainment of the level of Buddha Vajradhara in this very life. This is so because through the developing and fulfillment stages of *anuttaratantra* one realises the intrinsic emptiness and characteristic luminosity of mind and thus achieves the primordial wisdom of *mahāmudrā*, essence of enlightened vision.

With regard to the order of *vajrayāna* practice, one should firstly receive empowerment and maintain the appropriate *samaya*, and then practise the stages of meditation for which one has obtained authorisation in the empowerment. It is a fundamental prerequisite of *vajrayāna* practice that one must first have received empowerment (dbang), textual transmission (lung) and guiding instructions (khrid). As it says in the *Mahāmudrātilaka:* 'Without empowerment there can be no *siddhis* just as one cannot extract butter from sand'.[50]

Subsequent to having received empowerment, textual transmission and instructions, one must maintain the *samaya* vows and sacred pledges received at the time of the empowerment itself. In the *anuttaratantra* the most important *samaya* vows are embodied in the commitment to avoid the fourteen root downfalls which are:

> To disparage one's guru
> To contradict Buddha's word
> To be angry with vajra brothers and sisters
> To abandon love for all sentient beings
> To abandon the *bodhicitta*, root of *dharma*
> To disparage one's own and others' *dharma*
> To reveal secret teachings to those without empowerments
> To have contempt for the five psycho-physical constituents which are the five Buddhas
> To doubt that all phenomena are pure-beyond elaboration

To show love to harmful beings
To conceptualise the true nature of phenomena
which is ineffable
To disturb the faith of others
Not to rely on *samaya* substances at the time of the
circle of offerings
To despise women whose nature is wisdom

These *samaya* vows preserve the vision of sacred outlook
to which one is introduced at the time of empowerment.
Since one's guru is the root of *samaya* and thus the
object of the first of the fourteen downfalls, one needs
to be continually mindful that he is spiritually identical
with the deity of the empowerment and thus has the
stature of a Buddha. With this basic recognition of the
guru as Buddha, all aspects of the *samaya* vows will be
effortlessly maintained.

In the new *tantra* tradition as maintained by the
Sakya, Ngor and Tshar lineages, the chief practices of the
anuttara cycle are the six-limbed meditation of Śrī Hevajra and the developing and fulfillment stage meditation
of Vajrayoginī derived from the teaching of the *siddha*
Nāropā. In addition the Sakya school is famed as the
holder of the profound and esoteric teachings known as
the Thirteen Golden *Dharmas,* [51] which include not
only the meditation of Vajrayoginī already mentioned but
also the meditations of such deities as Śrī Jambhala and
Kurukulla whose practice bestows upon one beneficial
worldly powers like 'wealth-creation' and 'magnetising'.[52]

Furthermore the various lineages of the Dakpo Kagyu
uphold the custom of practising the preliminary and main
stages of their special transmissions of *mahāmudrā*
alongside meditation on such deities as Vajravarahi and
Cakrasaṃvara and the fulfillment stage yogas known as
the 'Six Doctrines of Nāropā'. Many Kagyu meditators also

maintain regular practice of the Chod precepts derived
from the lineage of Machig Labdron.

In the ancient tantra tradition of the Nyingma the
most profound of all *vajrayāna* teachings are the three
'inner yogas' of *mahā, anu* and *ati,* the practice of which
is prefaced by the accomplishment of the preliminary
meditations, most importantly *guru-yoga. Mahā-yoga*
consists of meditation upon Guru Padmasambhava in the
form of guru, deity and *dākinī* or upon such deities as
Vajrakilaya. The focus of *anu-yoga* is meditation upon the
subtle body of winds, channels and drops. Finally, in *ati-
yoga* one recognises and settles in the natural emptiness
of awareness through view, meditation and action.

Through the practice of these pure teachings of the
new or ancient *tantras* one will gather the two accumula-
tions of merit and primordial wisdom. Equipped with
these provisions for the spiritual journey one will swift-
ly traverse the five paths and ten *bodhisattva* stages[53] until one attains the level of a Buddha. Here the ocean of
birth and death has evaporated since its cause,
unawareness of the true nature of mind, has disappeared.
Mind's nature, emptiness and luminosity, stripped of its
obscurations is now resplendent as *dharmakāya* and
nirmāṇakāya and their union *sambhogakāya.* Thus the
basis, buddha-nature, the path, the development and
fulfillment stages, and the fruit, Buddhahood, possessing the three *kāyas,* are in truth grounded in the one
reality of mind, the union of luminosity and emtiness.

In enlightenment one is enthroned on the seat of Buddha Vajradhara, emperor of the diamond sky of ultimate
reality. Endowed with the Buddha-qualities of wisdom
that cognises thoroughly the nature of all phenomena,
compassion that embraces all without partiality and
power that is totally efficacious, one unceasingly and non-

conceptually achieves the benefit of all beings until the end of *samsāra*.

Completed by the layman Jampa Thaye on 3rd January, 1989, the anniversary of the Lord of **Dharma,** *Jamgon Kongtrul, with prayers that the glorious teachings of Buddha might spread throughout the world bringing joy and liberation to all beings.*

Seven

Notes

¹ Maitreya/Asanga, *Theg-pa Chen-po rGyud bLa-ma'i bsTan-bcos,* Rumtek, n.d. p.23a.

² In later Buddhist history, a number of different presentations of *Madhyamaka* have been transmitted, chief amongst which are the *rang-stong* ('empty of self'), and *gzhan-stong* ('empty of other') views which, although deriving ultimately from India received their most pronounced forms in Tibet. For *rang-stong-pa* thinkers, such as the Sa-skya-pa master bSod-nams Seng-ge and rDzogs-chen gZhan-dga' as well as numerous dGe-lugs-pa scholars, ultimate reality is emptiness beyond all elaboration. However, for *gzhan-stong-pas* such as Shākya mChog-ldan, Dol-po-pa Shes-rab rGyal-mtshan and Karma-pa Mi-bskyod rDo-rje, ultimate reality is actually the empty yet simultaneously luminous nature of mind beyond all extremes and thus inaccessible to conceptual elaboration and identical to buddha-nature, the potential for enlightenment inherent in all beings. Furthermore, whilst the *rang-stong-pas* hold the teachings of the 'second turning of the wheel' (q.v.) to be of definitive meaning (nges-don), and those of the third turning to be only provisional (drang-don), the *gzhan-stong-pas* though viewing the 'second turning' as comprising a mixture of provisional and definitive teaching, see the 'third turning' as totally definitive and therefore expressive of Buddha's highest teaching.

³ *Mahāmudrā* (phyag-rgya chen-po). In the new *tantra* schools *mahāmudrā* (literally 'great seal') denotes the realisation of primordial wisdom attained through the unification of the 'development' and 'fulfilment' stages of *anuttaratantra* practice.

⁴ *Ati* (mahāsandhi/rdzogs-pa chen-po), literally 'great perfection', is the key doctrine of the Nyingma tradition although it also has numerous adherents in the Kagyu and Sakya schools. According

to the *ati* perspective since all phenomena of *saṃsāra* and *nirvāna* are fundamentally empty they are perfect as they are. Liberation therefore occurs through recognition of, and settling in, this utter purity which is coextensive with awareness (rig-pa) the foundation of our being.

5 The 'Six Doctrines' most famous as the Six Doctrines of Naropa comprise the yogas of heat, illusory-body, luminosity, dream, transference and intermediate-state.

6 As quoted in Tsar-chen bLo-gsal rGya-mtsho, 'bShes-gnyen Dam-pa bsTen-par Byed-pa'i Thabs Shloka lNga-bcu-pa'i 'grel-pa dNgos-grub Rin-po-che'i sGo-byed,' in *Lam-'bras sLob-bshad*, Dehra Dun, 1986. Vol. nya p. 456.

7 *Id.*, p. 428.

8 For Tsar-chen's commentary see note 6 above. gZa'-dPal-sprul, *rDzogs-pa Chen-po kLong-chen sNying-tig gi sNgon-'gro'i Khrid-yig Kun-bzang bLa-ma'i Zhal-lung*, pub., Dingo Chentze, 1985. sGam-po-pa, *Dam-chos Yid-bzhin Nor-bu Thar-pa Rin-po-che'i rGyan* Rumtek, n.d.

9 Maitreya/Asanga, *op. cit.*, p. 4a.

10 See Note 1, above.

11 The *abhidharma* (chos-mngon) represents the collection of Lord Buddha's teachings on the constituent elements of the mental and physical realms. Knowledge of the *abhidharma* analyses and classifications of the five psycho-physical constituents (form, feeling, perception, formations and consciousness) the sense-bases and elements, provides the foundation for penetrating insight into the inherent emptiness of phenomena.

12 The *vinaya* ('dul-ba) is the collection of Lord Buddha's teaching on moral discipline for monks, nuns, laymen and laywomen.

[13] An *arhat* (dgra-bcom-pa). One who has gained the highest spiritual realisation available in the lesser vehicle, the culmination of the four stages of perfection: stream-entry, once-returner, non-returner and arhatship.

[14] A *bodhisattva*. One who has dedicated himself/herself to the achievement of Buddhahood for the benefit of sentient beings.

[15] The spiritual levels (Skt. bhūmi/Tib. sa) are the successive spiritual levels attained by *bodhisattvas* on the way to Buddhahood and are ten in number. Lord Buddha expounded the qualities and practices inherent in each level in the *Dasabhumikasūtra*. See also note 53 below.

[16] On those vows see Chapter VI.

[17] Śāntideva, *Byang-chub Sems dpa' sPyod-pa la 'jug-pa*, Rumtek n.d., pp. 15a-15b.

[18] Nāgārjuna, *Shes-pa'i sPring-yig*, manuscript copy.

[19] Śāntideva, *op. cit.* p. 9a.

[20] Thogs-med bZang-po, *rGyal-sras Lag-Len so-bdun-ma*, Shes-bya gSar Khang, n.d.

[21] As quoted in Ngor-chen dKon-mchog Lhun-grub, *Lam-'bras-sNgon-'gro Khrid-yig sNang-gsum mDzas-par Byed pa'i rGyan*, pub. Phende Rinpoche, New Delhi, n.d., p. 92.

[22] According to Lord Buddha, life begins at conception when the attaching consciousness from the intermediate state fuses with the sperm and ovum. Thus to take life by abortion, experimentation or so-called contraception that is in reality abortifacient is in *dharma* equal to any other form of killing (although of course genuine contraception which prevents the coming together of the sperm and ovum and thus does not draw in consciousness is permitted since no sentient being is killed). On this, Ngor-chen

Kun-dga' bZang-po declares in 'Zhen-pa bZhi-bral gyi Khrid-yig' (*gDams-ngag mDzod* Vol. 6, p. 332): 'Having produced the thought to kill which arises from any of the three poisons if you intentionally kill any living being — from an insect, like an ant up to a man or unborn child — then you have performed the act of killing'.

Furthermore, my own guru Karma Thinley Rinpoche has said (*Life News* no.19, 1988, pub. LIFE, Leamington Spa): 'When we go for refuge in the Buddha we also say that we will abandon harming sentient beings. It is for this reason that Buddha himself has expressly forbidden abortion — it is the taking of human life', and 'When people have abortions, they say that it is a small thing, and that it doesn't count, but this is a human being. They may be killing someone like Jetsun Milarepa or a universal emperor or even Buddha. You cannot throw human beings away like that. It is because abortion is such a great sin and such an evil action that the result of it can only be very great suffering'. In addition the great Karma-Kagyu scholar Khenchen Thrangu Rinpoche has declared (*The Open Door to Emptiness*, Lhundrup Teng. Kathmandu, 1978): '...once conception has occurred, to kill the foetus would be to destroy a sentient being, to commit an act of killing, and would be an unvirtuous action'.

For further details see my *A Circle of Protection for the Unborn*' Ganesha Press, Bristol, 1986.

[23] Nāgārjuna, *op. cit.*

[24] rJe-btsun Grags-pa rGyal-mtshan, 'Zhen-pa bZhi-bral', *gDams-ngag mDzod*, pub. Dingo Chentze, Paro, Bhutan, Vol. 6, p. 312.

[25] As quoted in Ngor-chen dKon-mchog Lhun-grub, *op. cit.*, p. 58.

[26] sGam-po-pa, *rJe sGam-po pa'i Zhal-gdams Lam-mchog Rinpo-che'i Phreng-ba*, manuscript copy, n.d.

[27] rJe-btsun Grags-pa rGyal-mtshan, *op. cit.* p. 313.

[28] Śāntideva, *op. cit.*, p. 3a.

[29] *id.*, p. 3b.

[30] *id.*, p. 13a.

[31] *id.*, p. 51b.

[32] *id.*, p. 54a.

[33] *id.*, p. 55b.

[34] rJe-btsun Grags-pa rGyal-mtshan, *op. cit.*, p. 313.

[35] See 'jam-mgon Kong-sprul in *gDams-ngag mDzod*, Vol. 4, pp. 243-275.

[36] Śāntideva, *op. cit.*, p. 45a.

[37] As quoted in Ngor-chen dKon-mchog Lhun-grub, *op. cit.*, p. 180.

[38] Candrakīrti, *dbU-ma la 'jug-pa*, Gangtok, 1979, pp. 12-13.

[39] Candrakirti, *id.*, p. 48.

[40] Śantideva, *op. cit.*, p. 59b.

[41] As quoted in Ngag-dbang Legs-pa, *'khor-'das dbyer-med gyi lta-ba'i snying-po bsdus-pa bkal-bzang gi bdud-rtsi*, manuscript copy.

[42] As quoted in Ngor-chen dKon-mchog Lhun-grub, *op. cit.*, p. 202.

[43] bSod-nams rTse-mo, 'rGyud-sde sPyi'i rNam-par gZhag' in *Lam-'bras Tshogs bShad* vol. *zha*, p. 543.

[44] 'jam-mgon Kong-sprul in Karma-pa Mi-bskyod rDo-rje *bKa'-brgyud mGur-mtsho*, Rumtek, n.d.

[45] Ngag-dbang Legs-pa, *op. cit.*

[46] As quoted in Ngor-chen dKon-mchog Lhun-grub, *Lam-'bras dNgos-gzhi'i Khrid-yig rGyud-gsum mDzes-par Byed-pa'i rGyan*, pub. Phende Rinpoche, New Delhi, n.d. p. 46.

[47] Mar-pa Lotsa-va in Karmā-pa Mi-bskyod rDo-rje, *op. cit.*, p. 64b.

[48] bSod-nams rTse-mo, *op. cit.*, p. 455.

[49] As quoted in Ngor-chen dKon-mchog Lhun-grub, *op. cit.*, p. 132.

[50] As quoted in Sa-skya Paṇḍita, *sDom-pa gSum-gyi Rab-tu dBye-ba'i bsTan-bcos.*, pub. Ngawang Topgyal, New Delhi, 1987, p.65.

[51] The 'Thirteen Golden *Dharmas*' are the deities Black Mañjuśrī, Vajra Garuda, Siṃhananda, Simhavaktra, Kurukulla, Kamarāja, Srī Jambhala, Ganesha, Vasudharinī, Indra Ḍākinī, Maitri Ḍākinī, Nāro Ḍākinī and Uma Devī.

[52] These are two of the four *Karmas* (activities): pacifying, wealth-creation, magnetising and destroying, through which a *tantric* yogin benefits the *dharma* and sentient beings.

[53] The five paths are accumulation, application, insight, meditation and beyond practice. The ten stages are the joyful, pure, illuminating, radiant, difficult to conquer, the one which is present, the far-going, the immovable, good mind and cloud of *dharma*. Both Sa-skya Paṇḍita in his '*Illuminating the Thought of the Sage*' (*Thub-pa'i dGongs-gsal*) and sGam-po-pa in his '*Ornament of Liberation*' provide extensive treatments of these topics.